HERE'S LOOKING AT YOU, WORLD!

POEMS BY LEWIS BROWN

Illustrations by Savannah Raines

Cover Design & Illustrations: Savannah Raines

ISBN: 978-1-959563-32-7

Published by:
Maudlin Pond Press
P.O. Box 53
Tybee Island, GA 31328
www.maudlinpond.com

Like gems washed by rain, Brown's poems radiate an inner light, a contentment born of seeing the world anew. He opens our "awes" as a boy watches lightning explode a palm that burns in the rain. Or as a man, seeing through a granddaughter's eyes as the sun dances through clouds. Through his tributes, we too, learn to pause and ponder when we might rush obliviously through life.

His gaze, seasoned by crossing borders and living among cultures, helps him create and play fresh new chords of joy and humor. Whether taking the "shortcut," or unplugging gutters full of sodden leaves that so often block currents of connection, he captures momentary beauty – an epiphany – that must be revered, observed, witnessed, and so he "scratched it down and put in my pocket." This practice surprises and excites our senses, helping us, too, to experience the world anew.

Faith Eidse – award-winning author of her memoir, Deeper than African Soil *(Masthof Press, 2023).*

Spontaneity and freshness, they are what strike me about Lewis Brown's poems. Simple themes that are much deeper than they seem at first reading. Lewis draws you into the moment just the way modern poetry calls for. Modern poetry calls for living in the moment, in what I like to term "dingly suchness." No need for allusions or moving outside the poem itself to grasp its meaning. Just being in the presence of the present. It's a pleasure experiencing Lewis's world of poems that reveal the depth of being there.

Will Strong – author of Connecting Reflections

FOREWORD

My poems capture how I see my world. As I observe and experience, I am often impressed with the exchanges between people and those around them, and the ways of the living earth and creatures around me.

I have been writing poems for years, capturing the moments while I worked, watching friends, family, and colleagues, noting an epiphany on a walk or in a quiet moment of observation. Sometimes it was all I could do to scratch down the verse and put it in my pocket.

This collection is framed around four themes: the seasons of the earth around us, the scenes that surprise us in daily life, moments of change, and ponderings. As I sorted and selected for this anthology, I had invaluable help from two important people in my life, my sister and my daughter. Their contributions in selection, revision, edits, and encouragement made this collection take shape.

Life in our world is exciting, funny, and constantly new. Of course, I notice the challenge, the horror, the fear, the inertia, and the entropy of things. These realities are not the focus of my writings. I am watching for the next steps toward an entirely new world.

I gratefully dedicate this volume to my life partner, Carolyn Elizabeth Freeman Brown.

Lewis Brown
2025

TITLE POEM

HERE'S LOOKING AT YOU, WORLD!

It's the time of year
When they show Casablanca. Again.

I was just returning from a stroll in a frigid world.
The last crunches of my boots
Were amplified by the concrete stairs.
Somehow there was a Sun,
A broken egg yolk in a pan of dark sky,
And it followed me through the door.
"Here's looking at you, Kid."
I heard the dialog streaming and I thought:
Bogart's poignant goodbye was
A memory AND a declaration of love.
'I loved you then, and I love you now.'

I looked out at the scramble in the afternoon sky,
Fried light framed by evergreens.
"Here's looking at You, World.
I loved you then, and I love you now."

INDEX OF POEMS

PART 1:
SEASONS CYCLING

SINGING "FALL!"

Little green factories at the end of a stem
All closing for the season.
Transformed without sap, they are green no more,
Splashes of red and gold falling with the rain
From gray sky to gray concrete
And the city gutters are awash.

In the afternoon,
Like stiff little colored cards, they blow along the
street,
Corners scraping with the music
Of the windy race across the sidewalks,
Until they gather in piles in the corners of our town
And sing together, "Fall!"

WATCHING IT BURN IN THE RAIN

It was a thing of wonder,
The storm coming through the night.
We felt it in the breeze
And smelled it, wet and pungent
Across the dark fields of grass.
We hurried home from the neighbors' house
Before the first drops hit the roof.

A brilliant flash, then
BOOM! the first thunder overhead
Filled our room as we dressed for bed.
We were too excited to sleep.

In the dark we watched:
Lightning, then thunder,
Followed by waves of rain,
Pelting the walls, driven by the wind.
Light and sound matched the rain
As the storm moved over us.

Then another flash
And we heard a crash across the road!
Lightning hit a palm tree.
We looked through the window in wonder,
And stared.
The palm tree was torn open
And it was burning in the rain.

FALL FLIGHT

The airport is a somber place
This evening travel day.
A busy collection of questers
Line up in jackets,
Then head down the corridor
Followed by their droning wheels.

Planes leave pink contrails in the dusk
As we travel into night.
Above us the endless,
And below us the homes
Closing up for the night.

The hums and hisses of the cabin surround us;
The lights dim and sleepers shuffle,
Turning in their seats and wrapping themselves in
rest.

Arrivers turn collars to the cold,
To the shadowed world studded with lights.
Clusters of people drag bags,
Half-awake, yawning in line,
Waiting for coffee along the walkways;
They study their phones for the real time.

We walk by on our way,
Heading for the luggage carousels,
And watching for family who wait there with hugs.

BOOT WEATHER

Frosted leaves and grass
Crush under boots newly rescued from storage.
Wool socks and big coats wrap us
But our noses chill in the air.

This morning walk shows our cloud breaths,
And we plosh, we scrunch,
We splunch through leaves
Along our trail to coffee and a warm room.

MOON IN THE MORNING

With a cold clear dawn
I found a full Moon
Resting on a powerline
Like a fat bird,
Pale in the rising Sun,
A fantastic creature
Flaked with frost
Fluffing feathers to keep warm.

PAINTED LEAVES

The color elves are out to play
I could tell the other day.
The trees had leaves with shades of fall,
Rainbow dancers big and tall.

The morning cold and morning breeze
Blew the leaves around my knees —
They scattered colors in the air,
Piling splotches everywhere.

Painted leaves flew into piles
Windblown colors bringing smiles —
The elves left colors for the air
To decorate the yards with flair.

BLOWN AWAY

Last night, It blew the moon away,
Gusting with a blustering breeze;
I know She did not want to go —
The moon grabbed onto trees!

That frowning disk of gloomy white
Tried hard to stop and stay,
But Pushy air just shoved and shoved,
And blew the moon away!

NOVEMBER MOON

Between the trees, the moon behold —
A dollop, bright and milky gold.
We stopped to gaze, this flare so bold —
In our view but moving on too soon.

Traffic crowds and rushes by,
Lights and sounds fill up the sky,
But for the moment, you and I,
We're gazing at the moon.

WINTER SUNLIGHT

My Christmas bulbs shine keenly in the early
morning pale;
Through the clouds, the puffy gray light
Seems eager to explore the dark places.

Then the dirty golden hints of day spread out
Coming through spaces between clouds and sky-
lines.
Streams of sun spill onto surfaces.
Winter rays angle beneath my bill—
Neither cap nor glasses can block them.
Even midday shadows are long,
And the light plays with shapes on the walls.

When I stand in the lingering winter light
The sunset breeze is cool and cryptic.
No colors stain the horizon as the sun packs up its
tools.
But the long tepid beams reassure me—
Everything is moving on.
Then the golden haze slowly fades into steel.

FIRESMOKE AT DUSK

I stopped among the trees
On a day between winter and spring,
And watched the fattening moon
Straddle barren branches.
I am chilled as the dusk drifts in,
The air scented with someone's firesmoke.

The coming night gathers up the twilight and flows
into the trees,
Leaving traces of light on the dark limbs
And filling the spaces with whispering gray.

I head home with my jacket pulled around my neck
And my breath hovering around my face;
I find my heart resting inside.

MARCH SUN

The March sun is cool,
But I come away from it warm.
I remember now:
The breeze cools the unsuspecting
And leaves them pink
After the sun has set.

I sit out watching the mountains
As if they will move, or grow,
And I smile
At the cloud feathers in the sky.

NIGHT RAIN

I woke to night rain,
Millions of drops landing in tandem
Drumming dozens of surfaces.

In the dark, it was the only sound.
The pounding on the grass resonates,
But on the roof and concrete it sounds uneven,
Spattering edges in batches;
Through my window I smile —
The warm room is a shelter of comfort.

Through a million lenses
The lone street light scatters light,
And reflections jump with each drop
On street and pavement.
Light follows sound at night —
I see what I think I hear.

I close the blinds
And lay down again in the dark,
And listen
To the night rain.

SUMMER

When summer comes
It is a warm surprise.
The bright mornings
Are early, and smiling.

It is good to see summer at first;
The pleasant days are fresh.
The humid heat has not grown tiresome,
And the long days are not boring yet.

Once summer moves in,
It takes over the front room.
It wants to dictate dinner,
And decide the movie for the night.

Summer is a party animal
Who doesn't want to be alone.
It is a house guest who laughs,
And makes us laugh at everything.

Summer is full of non-stop fun,
But does not let us rest.
I am glad to see it go,
But I am smiling as I wave goodbye.

FIRST AUTUMN RAIN

The first rain of Autumn came with the equinox.
A massive storm circled the coast slowly,
Clouds blew in and drained for hours.
The passing breezes did not chill me,
But the gusts reminded me to put away the summer.
I carried chairs in the drizzle,
Which left spatters on my clothes, the chairs and covers.

I held a cup of tea at the window and listened to the patter.
When I sat with a book, the couch felt comfier,
The lamp brighter, and the heavy socks warmer.

I was not sad, since I live with the rhythmic rotations:
The day and the night are twins today,
But in a few months the night will hog all the time.

Décor will change over the next weeks,
Events will take different shapes as we treasure the lights.
Coats will come out, short sleeves slide into drawers.
The shift of seasons brings days of transition,
Days of calendars and reviews.

But today, I embrace the change,
And watch the rain wash the roofs of leaves,
Watch the water gather in drains long dry,
And the wind wandering across soaked yards.

PART 2:
SCENES OF LIFE

SMIRKS AND GRIMACES

She sleeps on my lap,
This angel in onesies
Stretching and grunting in sleep.

She hears voices, and behind little lids
Her eyes move, and she rustles.

The banter and laughter of the house
Tickles the person inside her sleeping face
and she smirks, with a twist of expressive cheeks.

Then she stretches again and waves her arms
To clear the cobwebs around her head.

She shows a crooked smile while she sleeps.
She turns her head on my lap
when Dad comes by and kisses her,
and with a grimace she decorates her sleeping face.
After all, she is an angel in onesies.

PLAY DAY

She wakes up slowly, looking bright,
She's ready, since she slept the night.
She eats enough to fill both legs,
And when it's gone, "Some more" she begs!

Crawling, standing, almost walking,
Word-like sounds, she's almost talking.
Sparkling eyes and rosy cheeks,
When she between her fingers peeks:
"Where's the Mommy?" seems to say,
"And what's next on this play day?"

She grabs, she crawls, she stands, she cries,
She waves hello, she waves goodbye,
She shakes and chews, she flips and flings,
And wants the phone each time it rings.
She'll nap enough to keep on going,
Down for a while, then up and rolling.

Another show, another book,
Somewhere else she wants to look.
Some games, some hugs and then some more,
Some wandering all around the floor;
And when it's time to bathe and bed
She'll want to play some more instead.
But when at last play day is done,
She sleeps, my little funny one.

MUSTACHE

I picked him up to say goodbye
And got a big hug.

As I spoke to him, he looked at me closely,
And had to reach an index finger
To touch, so tentatively.
"Soft," he said slowly.
"Do you know what that is?"
"It's called a mustache," I said.
And he looked at me carefully,
And smiled.

NOISES IN THE HOUSE

The lady with the smiling eyes
Moves from room to room and peeks
Into closets, behind doors.

She hunts, then finds some joyful shrieks,
Little men glad to be found,
Grandsons playing hide and seek.

MORNING CROOKS AND NANNIES

She studied her muffin in earnest consternation.
"Mommy, it has holes in the bread."
"Yes, dear. Those are the nooks and crannies
For the butter and jam."
She looked at the butter dish
And back at the muffin.

Dad walked into the kitchen,
Dressed for work.
He kissed his daughter.
"Good morning my Muffin.
How are you?"

She looked up earnestly.
"Daddy, do all muffins have crooks and nannies?"

TIME FOR TINES

Across the table my little friend struggled.
The pieces were too long for the spoon,
And his many efforts could not capture them.
Finally, a gap-toothed grin looked up at me.
"I cam catchem!" He shared with anguish.

"Let's try a fork," I suggested,
And provided the young hunter
With a multi-tined stabbing tool.
The gap-toothed grin took it eagerly.
"This is different from the spoon.
You poke the food and pick it up," I explained.

The first piece was quickly conquered,
And in that moment I saw
The ancient hunter on the plains,
Spearing his prey with prowess.

He looked up with excitement,
And after stabbing his next piece,
He glanced at me mid-chew
With gratitude.

SUNNY CLOUDS

She carefully clicked her seatbelt,
And looked out of the window.
Her curls shook as she looked up—
Her eyes widened slowly.

She scanned her sky.
I could see her wonder—
"How are there sunny clouds?"
Her clear voice enunciated carefully.

I grinned and I looked again.
"Yes, the Sun is dancing
Through the clouds.
That's how you get
Sunny clouds."

SOCCER LEG

My friend sat down and smiled.
"I am here to tell you what happened,"
He announced proudly.
"We won; yes, we won!"

"We won the game?"
I asked excitedly.
I would have jumped up,
I would have danced and cheered!
But the cast on my leg felt funny.

LOVE MANGLES MY VISION

She was my best girl,
Intense and steady,
Warm and bright,
And determined to stick with me.

Of course, we had to make out,
So we wandered into the warm night,
Embracing and talking,
And found a spot behind her place.

Her dog Badge found us kissing in the grass,
Licked us both and made us laugh.
To do real kissing takes a free face,
So I took off my glasses, and she did as well.

I put my lenses on the dark grass
And turned to smooch my girl.
Badge lay down to watch and needed to chew.
My lenses. Plastic frames are crunchy.

FIVE O'CLOCK SHADOW

The April full moon flooded outside my room;
Through my window, the yard is a pool of white.
In the cool pre-morning
A young tree throws a full shadow
Across the white puffs of pale grass.

I am up for the day,
Ahead of the sleepy working sun.
As I pull out my shaver, I grin—
I see my yard has a five o'clock shadow, too.

GROWING STONES

I think my yard is growing stones;
I'm shoveling up the beds,
I'm looking for a place to grow
And finding rocks instead.

I wonder why they are in groups
When they come up from dirt.
Do shovels bother groups of stones?
Can sunlight make rocks hurt?

Do stones make more, and multiply?
And do they mate for life?
If they do, I just split up
The rock man from his wife.

THE "LONG CUT"

Driving where I do not live,
Encircling my goal,
Besieging it from nearby streets
And losing self-control.

The map is telling little lies—
This street does not go through!
And when I think I'll try the next
That road's a dead end, too.

And so the clever little way
I started out to take
Has got me taking extra miles;
The "short cut" is a fake!

TIGERS IN THE TREES

Walking home from school one day
I'm sure that it saw me,
I'm certain that I saw
A tiger in that tree.

Branches of our towering trees
Still bare from winter's shove,
So, for sure, you'd see his stripes
There crouching up above.

Tigers won't eat people
Walking near a traffic jam,
So, I doubt those striped hunters
Know exactly where I am.

Still, I think my worried self
Would feel more at ease,
If I could just be certain
Of no tigers in the trees.

ON THE FENCE

They are both on the fence,
And cannot decide.
It is a face-off,
Calling to each other in angry tones.

From my window I couldn't quite hear,
But it seems to be a squabble over details.
His head is bobbing up and down, pause, then
again,
And her head shakes and shakes,
Disputing but not deciding.
Then silence.
One more outburst.
Then, wings flapping,
They both flew off the fence with loud caws.

JUST LIKE US

"He smiles just like you do,"
She said with a grin
That looked much like her mother's own.
"And his fingers, look!"
She said, placing his tiny hand in mine.
I recognized my hands…
And I pondered it.

The generations before me —
Someone had his smile,
Someone had our hands.
Another mom grinned like that
In our distant past.

They really aren't "my" genes,
It's just that I am here to see
This little one arrive.

But… it is fun to be part of the lineage.

THE VENDING MACHINE

It was the fourth hour of sitting,
Waiting on awkward chairs.
Water, we must have some water.
But where?
The attendant at the desk
Sent me to the cafeteria on the second floor,
Next building, main corridor.
"I will find us water," I said.
I climbed stairs in search of bottles.
Of course, the cafeteria was closed. Very closed.

I saw vending machines, and one offered water.
I put in my bill. B6. Selection empty.
Try B1, I said to myself. It worked! A bottle.
The machine decided I was done.
Time for my change to be dispensed.
IN QUARTERS. All quarters.

But not in a change bowl — not into a receptacle.
No, they came shooting out about knee high.
Three dollars and seventy-five cents.
In quarters.
I was diving, grabbing, trapping,
As they scattered across the floor.
They were rolling into the walls,
Between my legs, bouncing with clinks.
I sat on the floor with my change. And a bottle.
And started to laugh. What a day.

I REMEMBER

A glare of afternoon sun
Suddenly slips from behind the cedar,
And fills the window.

Many times, I have averted my eyes
From a glare like this,
And I am remembering —
Sunlight in my eyes,
Days with friends.
Afternoons on the beach,
Or on a hillside,
On a park bench
Sharing a table and a talk
With those in my memory.

Some of them have gone,
But I carry a bit of them,
An expression, an idea, a passion.
Others I cannot see anymore.
We are in disparate places now.
Yes, I remember,
And despite the years and the decades passing,
Some parts don't fade.

The memories help, but those times aren't now,
And they can advise me,
But they don't direct me.

While I stand
I am facing forward,
And the memories that live
Help me complete THIS day.

PART 3
CHANGE MOMENTS

CHANGED IN A RELATIONSHIP

Cleaning windows on a sunny day,
She was inside, I was outside.
Sometimes I saw her, and smiled,
I teased, and sprayed her face in the glass.
Sometimes I saw me, although
I was brighter, with a glow in the sunlight.
Sometimes the sunlight was all that reflected.

And I thought for a moment about those comments
folks made:
"I hope you can live with her as she is. She won't
change."
"He will always be that way. He's not going to
change, you know."

Yet in the years since then,
I have become some of her,
And she some of me.

We did change.
By choosing each other.
By choosing oneness again and again.

IMMIGRANTS NO MORE

The war had taken their Papa away,
Then Granddad died another sad day.
Mom and young ones were left all alone,
Hard work to do, large bills to pay.

Family was distant, beckoning please,
Travel to places over the seas.
"Sell what we've got, pack it all up,
Buy our way over, pay all the fees."

November trip in the cold and the wet,
Cross the Atlantic, feeling regret,
Mother and young adrift in the new,
Out of detention, to family they went.

Wisconsin had snow and the home of a cousin,
But it was too cold and very closed in,
The brave little souls took a long trip,
Traveled by road to find other kin.

They found a church and some Cornish folks,
They could share songs and old Cornish jokes.
Mother watched children put roots and stay
Not straying too far from the old Cornish oaks.

As the time passed, new roots start to feed,
Each one grew older; they shared when in need.
Until their hearts were migrants no more,
No more "old country," they'd gone to seed.

SHE DANCES IN THE SUN

We arrived to a crowd gathered in the humid African heat,
A familial and a formal affair with official greetings,
And I, the eldest son, stood with my father
To receive the welcome and the handshakes.

Many others stand by as they wait to grasp a hand,
And I join my father as he greets the dignitaries.
Then the music begins, drums and singing,
And the others in the crowd dance with joy.
I accompany my father,
But she, she dances.

She dances with her people in the sun,
And the drums and voices are for her,
And surround her with joy.

The men shake hands, old friends embrace,
The family hugs, and talks, and laughs,
And she knows they must.

But in that moment, she is home,
And she, she dances with her people in the sun.

JUST UP THE TRAIL

My Dad has passed
And joined his brothers.
I envision it this way:

We were striding up a mountain trail,
And turned on a switchback.
We stopped to adjust our backpacks,
And I noticed the magnificent forest view.

I looked out, and down into the canyon.
I stopped, taken by the view far below.

Ahead of us, the trail turned steep
And curled around the mountain.
Dad went on ahead with his steady pace,
His shoes crunching the fallen leaves.

As I started to climb again
I heard voices laughing up the trail,
And I recognized my uncles' tones.
I could just hear their voices ahead,
Men enjoying each other's company.

And then my grandfather's voice
Came amidst greetings and laughter:
"Son, there you are!"

Yes, my father is just up the trail.

FISHING ON THE OTHER SIDE OF THE LAKE

"I'm going to try
The other side of the lake," he said.
He handed me one of his lures.
"Try this on them this morning.
Get it out there and reel in slowly."
A glance and a grin,
And we parted ways among the rocks.

Fishing in clear waters
On that mountain morning,
I notice him across
The wind-rippled surface,
And he is calling.
"... .Better spot... .400... over... "
He is pointing down the lake.
I get up and wave back.
I am climbing over granite boulders
To reach that better spot.

That's what uncles do.
They share their best lures.
They make sure you know
Where to be enjoying life.
They boldly live their faith.
They look you in the eyes,
And grin. "Now you do it."

HER FATHER'S EYES

We had grown together and I knew her well,
But that day I looked
Into her father's eyes —
Blue grays piercing through laugh lines,
A sparkling in her smile.

Although he was gone,
He was there —
The one I loved, respected, valued, missed.
She carried him in her eyes,
Her father's eyes.

MOVING IN: A MEMORY

The wedding was one thing, but
I remembered the moment I moved in
That early Fall Day —
A few possessions in drawers,
A toothbrush on the counter.

My excited grin grew
As you made room for me,
A roommate for life.

GRAND FATHER

Grandfather indeed!
Does that mean I am
Only a part of history,
A name in a long line;
Holding hands with the past
And with the future?

Are they extensions of decisions made long ago,
The results of what I did years earlier?
No... No...
Even if I had planned it all,
These little living histories
Take shapes I never could have foreseen.

They have come through me,
But I only share their lives.
And they will need me. Grandfather...

NEW AGAIN

I opened the front door to the August air
And stood in the doorway at twilight.
Once again, I was 21,
Before the children
And the jobs,
Before the routines
Of work and parenthood.
It was just you and me,
And I had just graduated.
I had found my life,
And was about to live it.
It feels that way
Again.

REACHING

Far it was
To where we were going,
And we arrived overnight.
We got up to see the dawn
From open sills
And reach into the morning light.

Then we touched the cool of ocean breath
And walked the dampened sand.
On a rock we dangled feet
In low tide surf
Sitting hand in hand.

HE IS GONE

On a beautiful evening,
As the Sabbath started,
He left.
He had taken some time to say goodbye;
He waited patiently
While the rest of us came to see him,
And then
He left.

He told me he was going, and that
He was ready to go.
I trust the timing of his departure,
But I am mourning.

We loved each other
Even though we were so very different.
So I cry
Not because we were close,
But because we came to trust each other.

We bypassed history and conquered fear,
And we trusted each other.

PART 4:
PONDERINGS

ON THE EDGE

Suddenly I was at the edge
And looked over.
The water glistened in the half-Sun
And the breeze pushed up the cliff
Over the edge, into my face.
I took one more step to look down
At the water's edge,
Lapping at the rocks far below.

What is it about the top of a cliff?
I won't fall over, but my pulse jumps.
Is it the physical change,
An abrupt shift in the land, water, sky?

Perhaps because here your footsteps stop.
You must face the change and adapt,
For you cannot continue the way you came.

It is intriguing that here,
On the cliff, we stop and study
Our surroundings, our past, our future.

ALL THE WAY

When it begins
You never think it will take everything.
You are willing to do your part,
But you are facing the demands of destiny.

Great conflict, and you are in the middle
Sitting in a dirty place with a weapon and a will,
A team of friends, and a load of fear.

The chaos of war galls the senses
And everything tries to confuse you,
But you force yourself to focus
And fight for the others
When you won't for yourself.

Others die and you are left.
You did nothing to be the one alive,
And the dead are better than you are.
What does it matter?
You are here, and you don't have time
To think about why.

The thunder comes in
And you move on.
You are taking land
Just to survive.

You lose men you didn't get to know
And you can't see the others who are with you.
You fight to control your fear
Because you are no good dead.

Stay with the orders
Stay with the job
This is no time to rethink your commitment.

War? I have known him.
Brother to Death and Chaos,
Father to Destruction.
The process of redemption is happening
While you hold insanity at bay.

BORN AGAIN (RENEWED AT THE RIVER)

We follow the humid pathway
Over packed sand between the high brush,
And the trail rolls down to the water.

The sky is gray but not heavy,
And the smells and sounds are muted.
The river is low and silent,
Creeping past the mud on the banks.

The splash of our feet
Into the tan stream surprises me,
But it does not echo.

The shallow water flows
Around my waist,
And I walk out to the sand bar.

For a moment I am young again
And the wonder of the browns,
The sand and the water,
The decaying leaves and sodden wood,
My damp hair, my companion's skin,
And the canoe against the bank,
Wraps me in the comfort
Of the cradle.

TO THOSE OF YOU WHO'VE FALLEN

To those of you who've fallen
And now will weep no more,
Those who shared our soil,
Whose roots have touched our Core:
You are now embedded
Where many others grow;
The rains still fall upon you,
Past you a bright wind blows.

Others grow beside you,
Your strength somehow they know,
The future is created
From seeds that you have sown.

DRY BED

Silent river stones litter the sand,
Scrawny bristles of brush line the edges,
A powdery trail wanders the center,
But no water.

The bed awaits. Clouds ignore.
The desert river doesn't run or ripple —
A sand channel where water would flow IS DRY.

Why does the river keep the bed made up?
Is the deluge dropping in?
Soon?

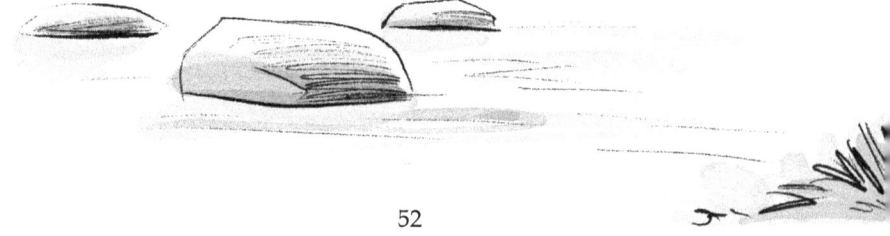

A PART, OR APART?

On a side track,
I spot a rusting freight car.
It stands alone in a tall grass field,
And I wonder why.

Where is his train?
Why was he left?

Useless in the sun
(Unless he is blocking the prairie wind).
He is storing air and bugs
Behind his rusted lock,
And he rots slowly in the field.

Illinois Central rolls by in the distance
Whistling as it passes, calling again.
Apart?
Or a part?

THE CURRENTS CONNECT US

The rain filled up the yards,
Streams poured from our roofs,
And ran down driveways.
The flat part of town flooded —
Every gutter overflowed.

I glanced outside — the entire street was stopped.
The storm wind filled our yards
With leaves blown from our trees,
And dams of leaves formed,
Every gutter flooded along the curb,
Blocked by the trash bins along the street.

I put on my boots and went out to get soaked.
I moved bins out of the gutters,
And swept away piles of sodden leaves.

I moved down the street to release each pool,
Sweeping the neighbors' gutters clear.
The pools of water hurried down the street.
The water moved along the curbs,
Grateful for the chance to flow again.

I stood in the rain and looked down the street,
My hat dripping just beyond my nose.
I watched the pools empty along the curbs.

We each had a leaf dam.
Yes, my curb becomes your curb,
And my pool runs into yours.
I saw it in that moment:
The currents connect us all.